### Hal·Leonard®
# KEYBOARD
## PLAY-ALONG

# BILLY JOEL
## HITS

cover photo © Ebet Roberts

In Australia Contact:
**Hal Leonard Australia Pty. Ltd.**
4 Lentara Court
Cheltenham, Victoria, 3192 Australia
Email: ausadmin@halleonard.com.au

ISBN 978-1-4234-4963-8

Visit Hal Leonard Online at www.halleonard.com

### HAL·LEONARD®
CORPORATION

7777 W. BLUEMOUND RD. P.O. BOX 13819

# BILLY JOEL HITS

## CONTENTS

| Page | Title | Demo Track | Play-Along Track |
|------|-------|-----------|------------------|
| 4 | Allentown | 1 | 2 |
| 11 | Just the Way You Are | 3 | 4 |
| 20 | New York State of Mind | 5 | 6 |
| 30 | Pressure | 7 | 8 |
| 39 | Root Beer Rag | 9 | 10 |
| 49 | Scenes from an Italian Restaurant | 11 | 12 |
| 65 | She's Always a Woman | 13 | 14 |
| 70 | Tell Her About It | 15 | 16 |

# Allentown

Words and Music by
Billy Joel

*Ending*

Hey, hey, hey. O, whoa, ho.

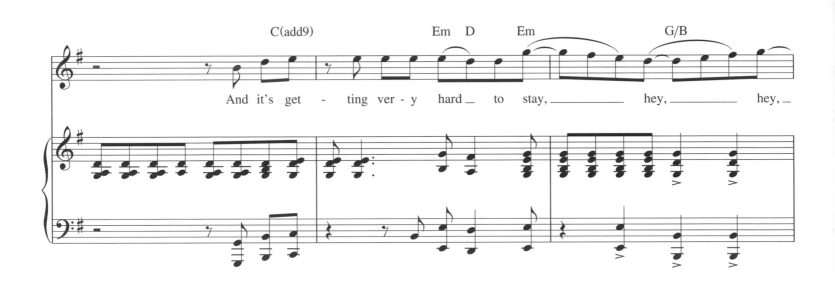

And it's get - ting ver - y hard __ to stay, _____ hey, _____ hey, _

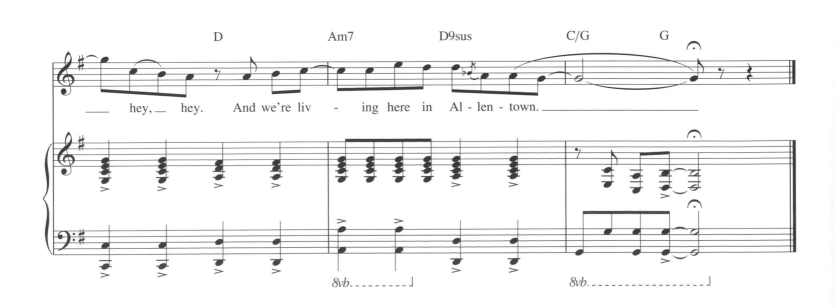

__ hey, __ hey. And we're liv - ing here in Al - len - town. _____

# Just the Way You Are

Words and Music by
Billy Joel

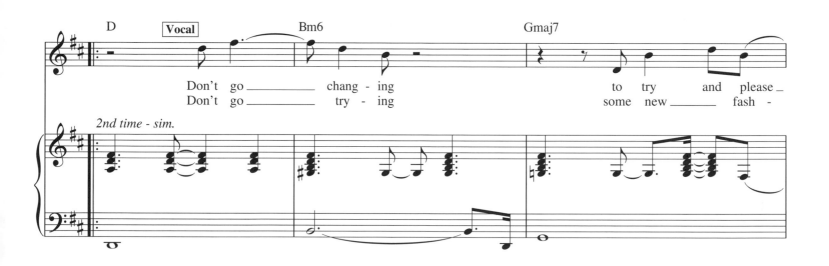

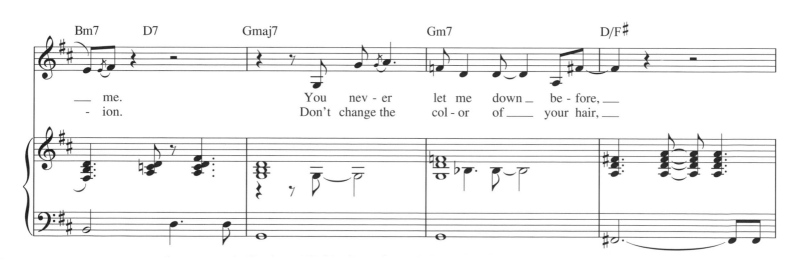

till you __ be - lieve __ in __ me __

the way that I _____ be - lieve _ in ___ you? I _____

**CODA**

*Sax solo*

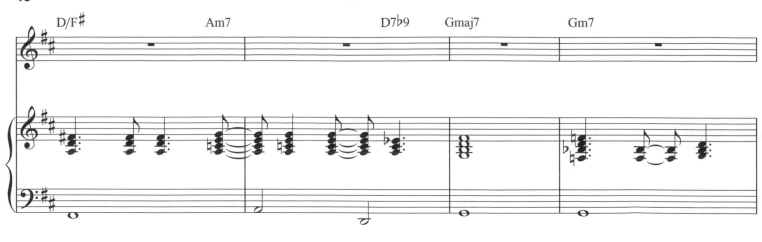

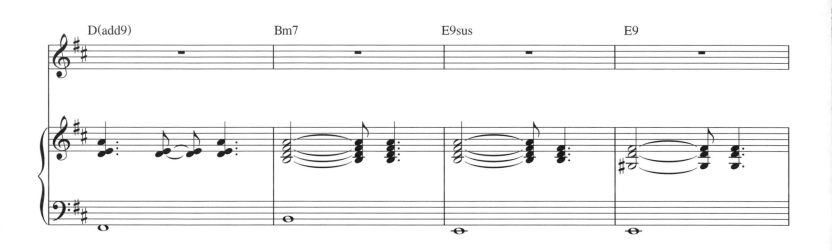

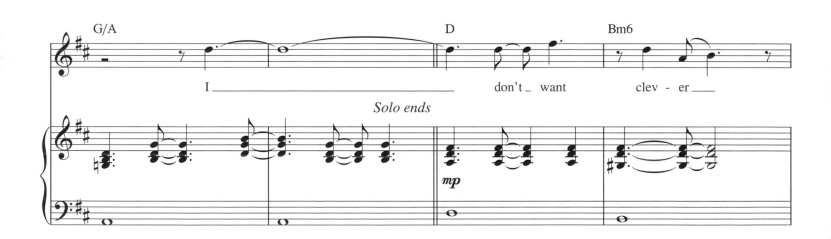

I _____ don't \_ want clev - er \_\_\_

*Solo ends*

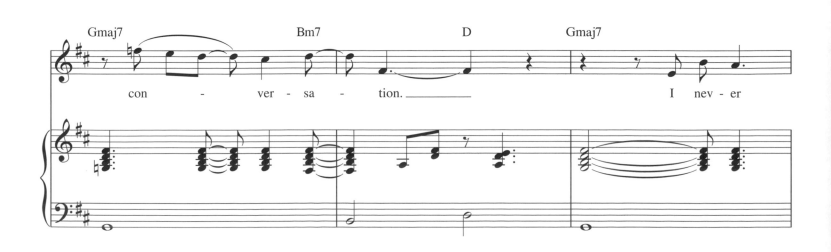

con - ver - sa - tion. _____ I nev - er

# New York State of Mind

Words and Music by Billy Joel

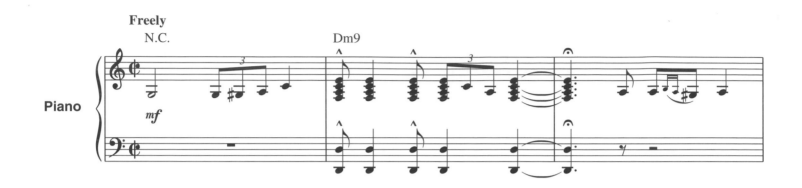

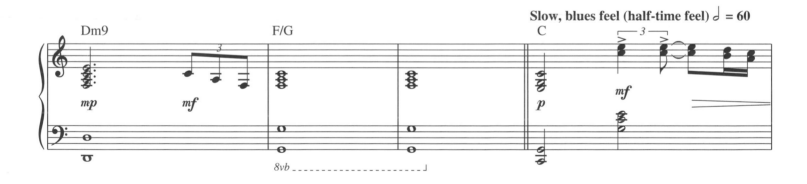

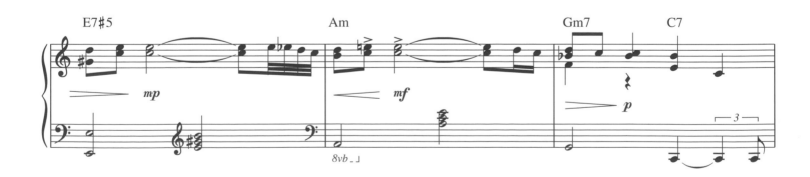

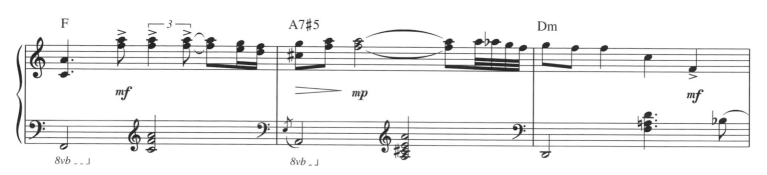

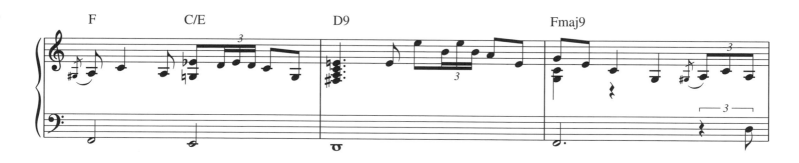

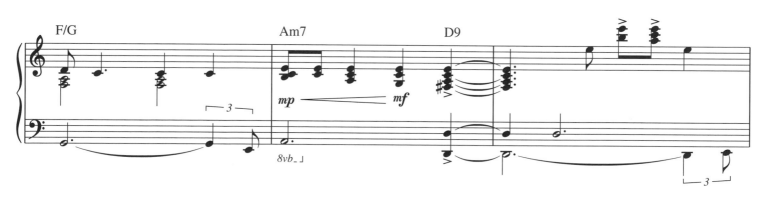

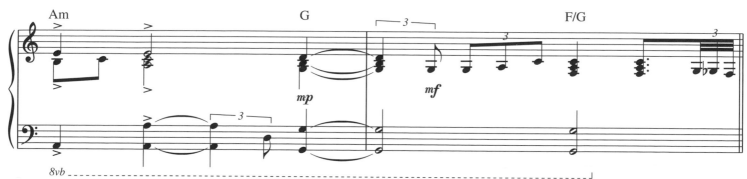

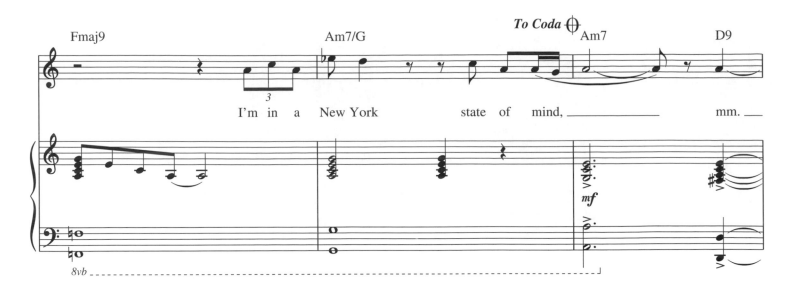

I'm in a New York state of mind, _____ mm. ___

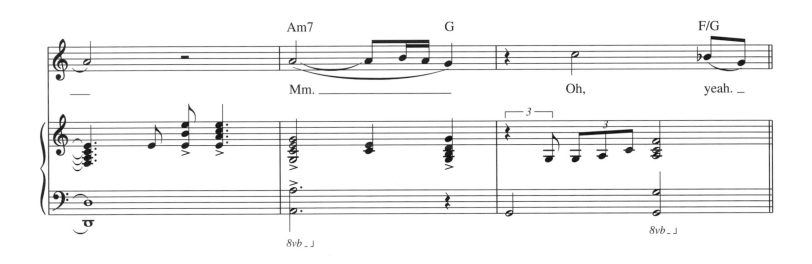

Mm. _____ Oh, yeah. _

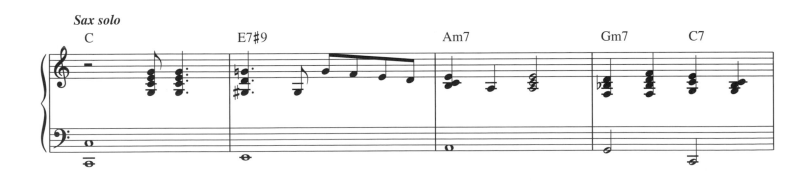

**Sax solo**

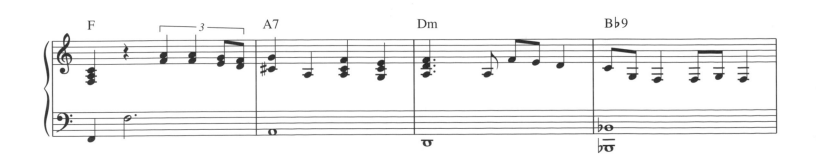

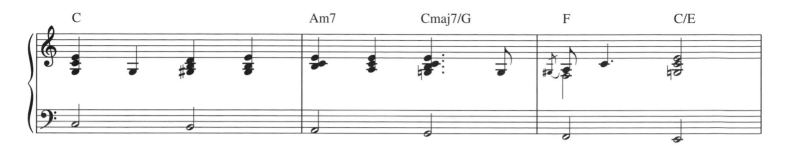

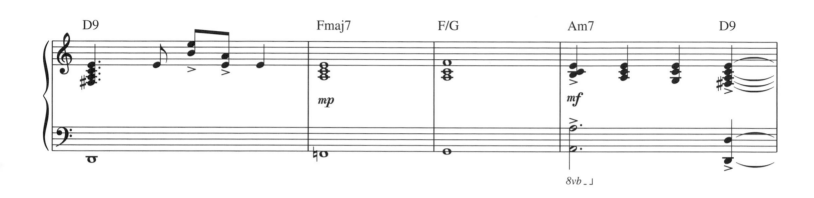

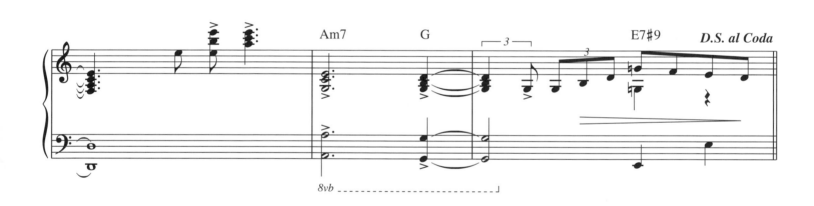

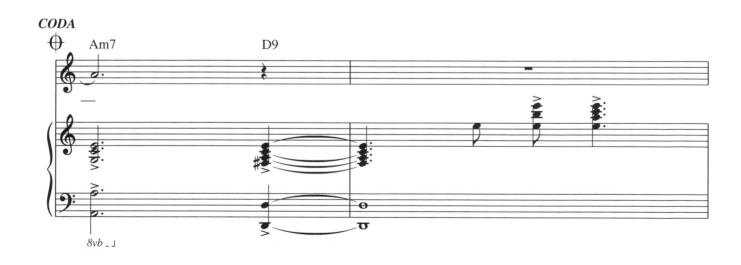

# Pressure

Words and Music by
Billy Joel

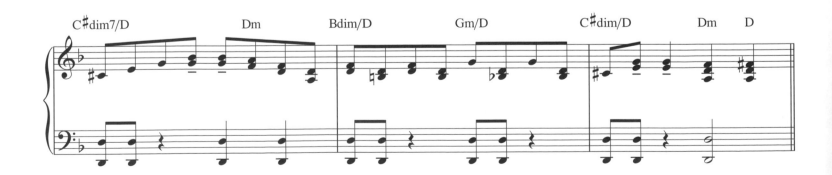

but you \_ will come to a place \_ where the on-

-ly thing \_ you feel \_ are load-ed guns in your

face and you'll have to deal \_ with pres-sure. \_

*Vocal 3rd time only* \_ \_ \_ \_ \_ \_ \_ \_ \_ \_ \_

Mm, \_

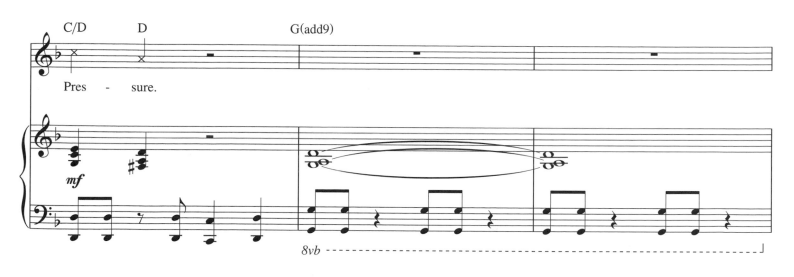

Pres - sure.

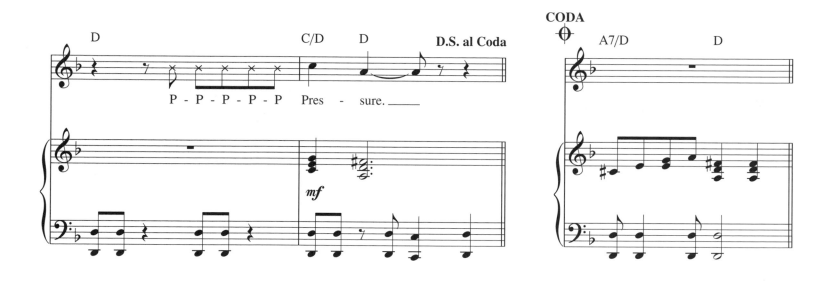

P - P - P - P - P   Pres - sure. ____

**D.S. al Coda**

**CODA**

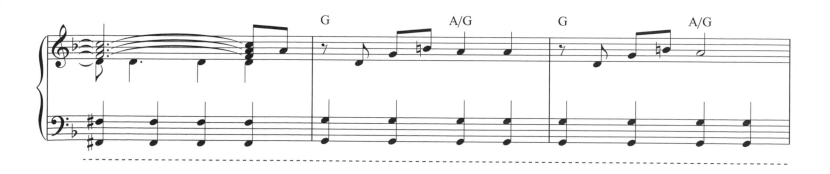

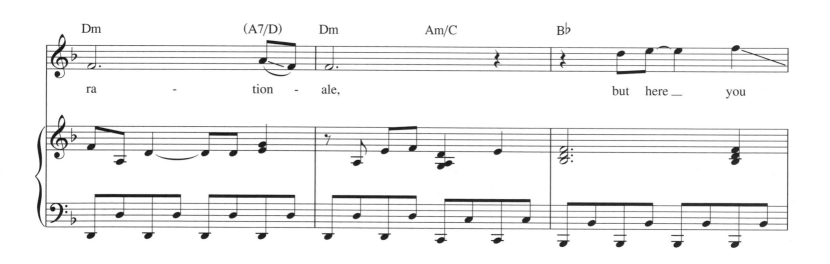

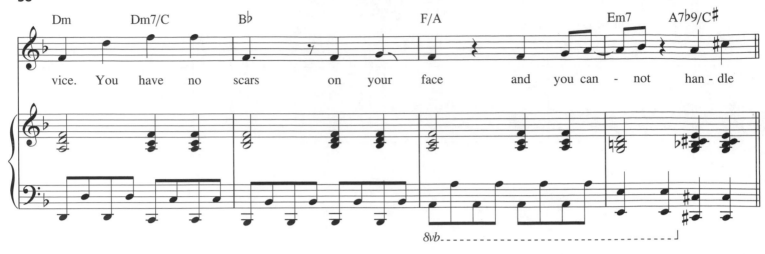

vice. You have no scars on your face and you can - not han - dle

pres - sure.

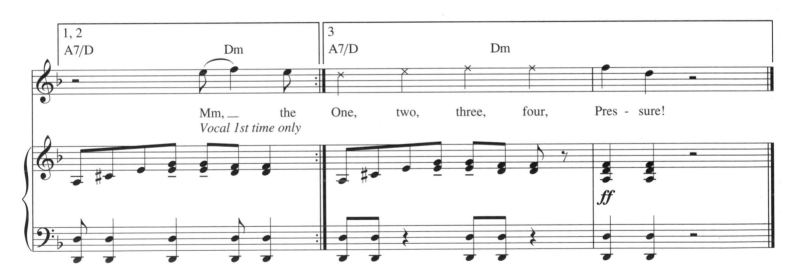

Mm, ___ the One, two, three, four, Pres - sure!

*Vocal 1st time only*

*Additional Lyrics*

2. You used to call me paranoid.  Pressure.
   But even you cannot avoid pressure.
   You turned the tap dance into your crusade.
   Now, here you are with your faith and your Peter Pan advice.
   You have no scars on your face and you cannot handle pressure.

3. Don't ask for help.  You're all alone.  Pressure.
   You'll have to answer to your own.  Pressure.
   I'm sure you have some cosmic rationale,
   But here you are in the ninth, two men out and three men on.
   Nowhere to look but inside, where we all respond to pressure.

# Root Beer Rag

Music by Billy Joel

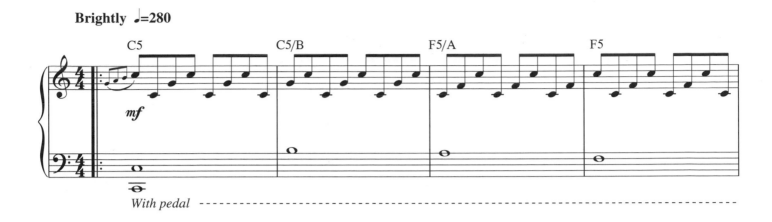

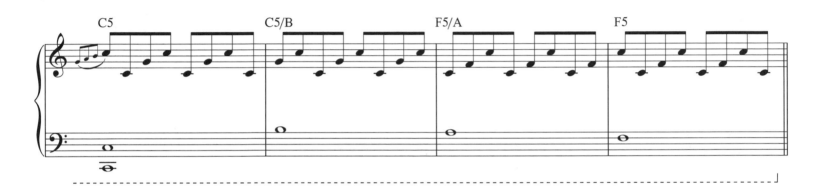

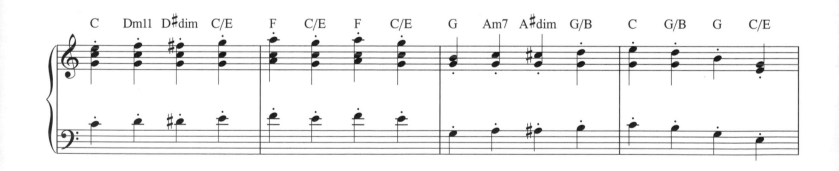

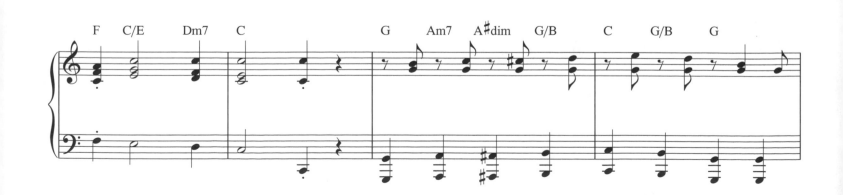

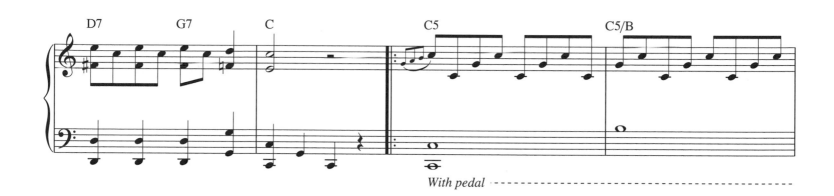

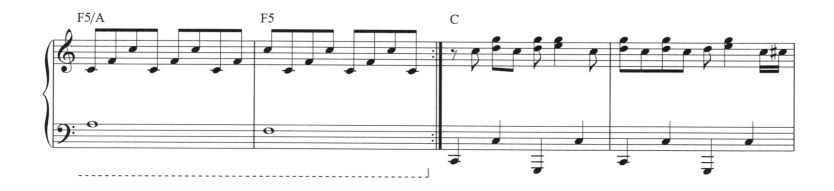

*With pedal* - - - - - - - - - - - - - - - - - - - - - - - - - - - - - - - - - - - - - - - - - - - - -

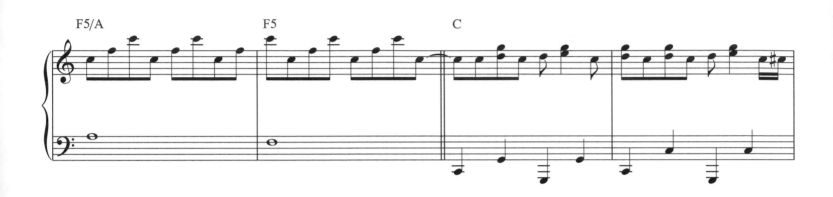

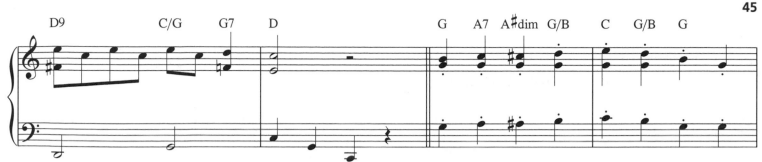

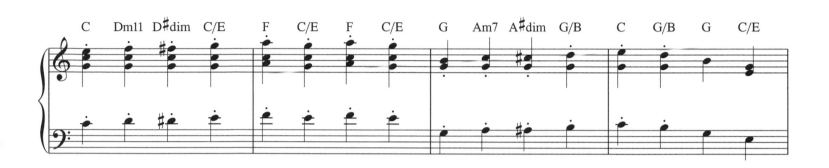

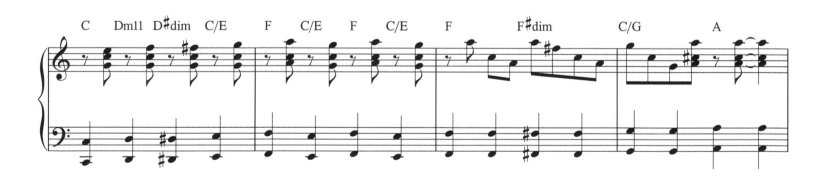

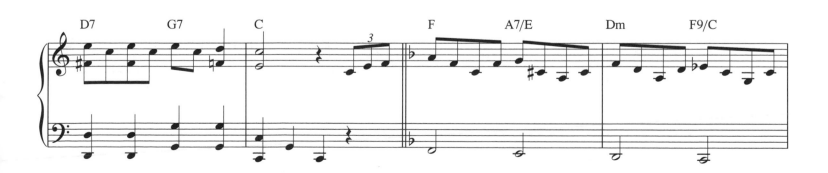

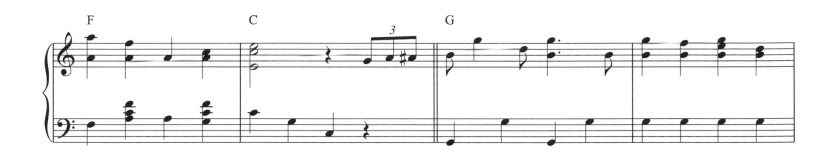

*With pedal* - - - - - - - - - - - - - - - - - - - - - - - - - - - - - - - - - - - - - - - - - - - - - - - - - - - - - - - - - - - - - - - - -

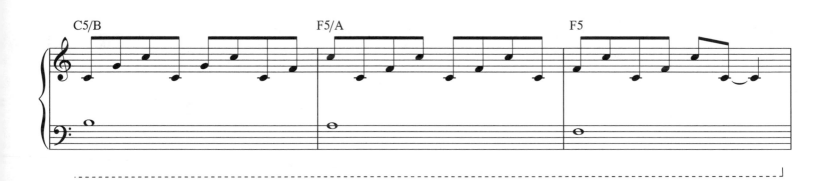

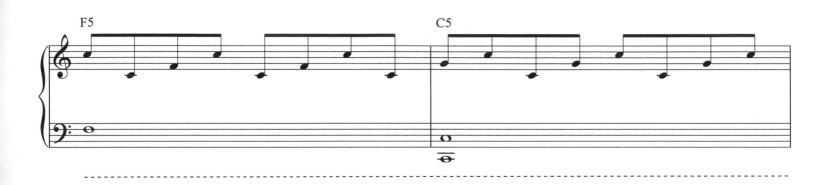

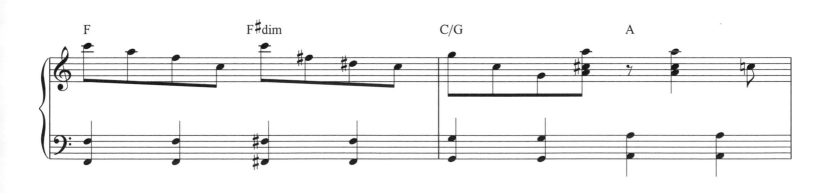

# Scenes from an Italian Restaurant

Words and Music by Billy Joel

- tau - rant. ___

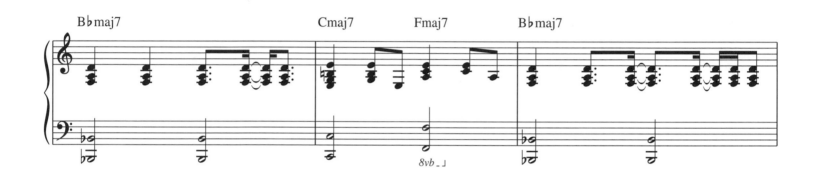

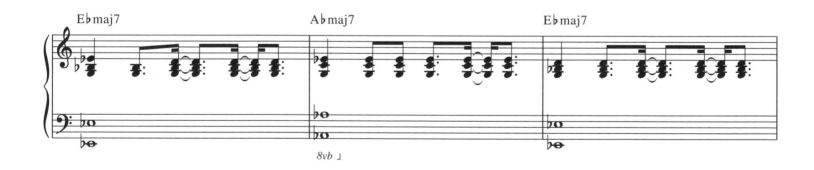

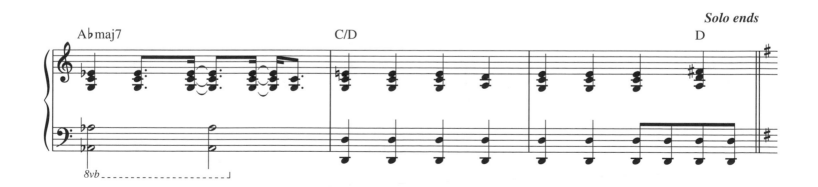

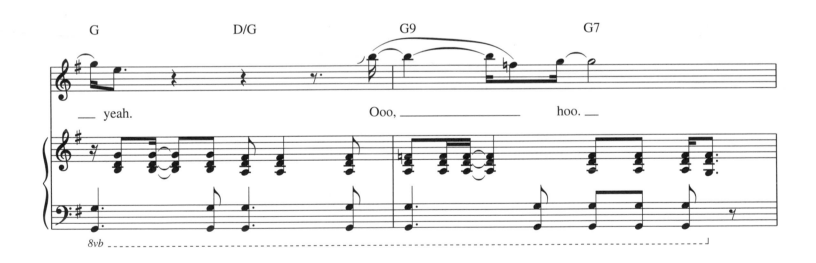

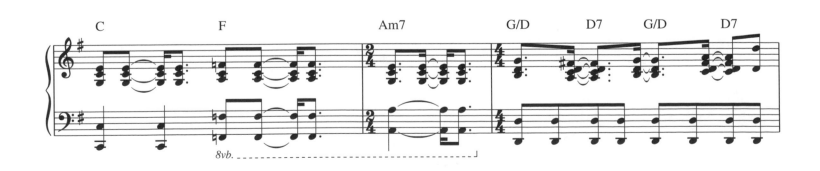

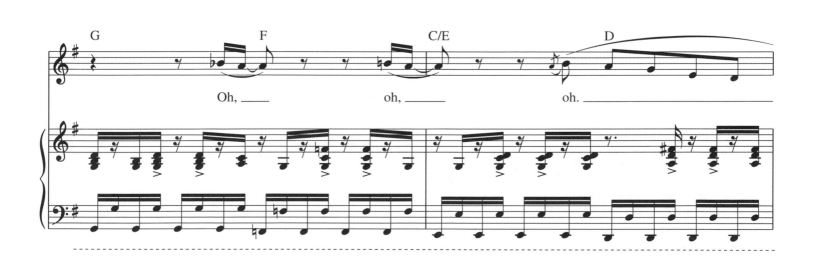

Oh, _____ oh, _____ oh. _____

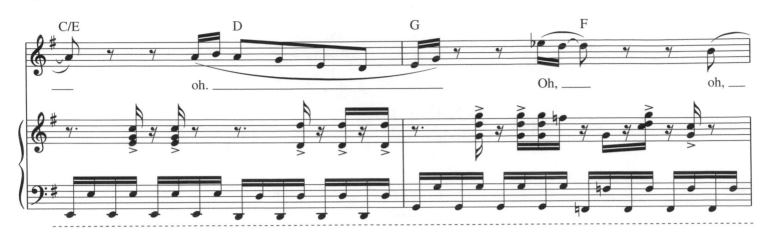

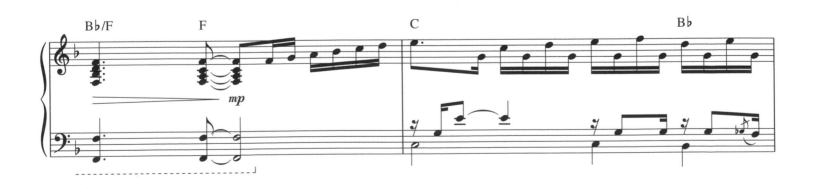

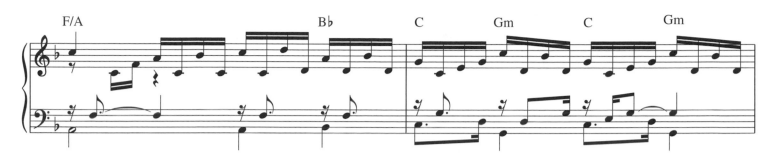

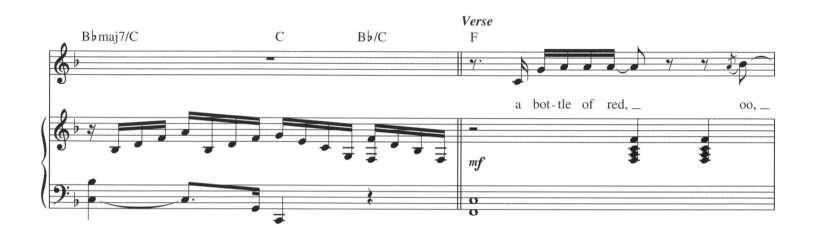

*Additional Lyrics*

2. Brenda and Eddie were still going steady in the summer of seventy-five
   When they decided the marriage would be at the end of July
   Everyone said they were crazy
   "Brenda, you know that you're much too lazy" and
   Eddie could never afford to live that kind of life.
   Oh, but there we were waving Brenda and Eddie goodbye.

3. Brenda and Eddie had had it already by the summer of seventy-five
   From the high to the low to the end of the show for the rest of their lives.
   They couldn't go back to the greasers
   Best they could do was pick up their pieces and
   We always knew they would both find a way to get by, oh and *(To Coda)*

# She's Always a Woman

Words and Music by
Billy Joel

me. She can lead you to love. ___ She can take you or leave you. She can

ask for the truth, ___ but she'll nev - er be - lieve _____ you and she'll

take what you give her _____ as long as it's free. Yeah, she

steals like a thief _ but she's al - ways a wom - an ___ to me. _____

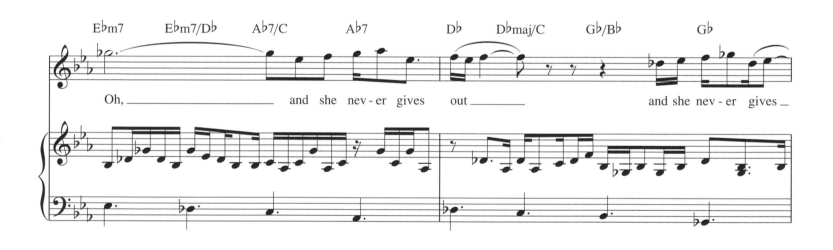

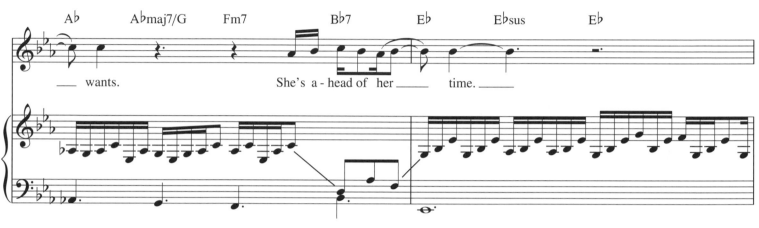

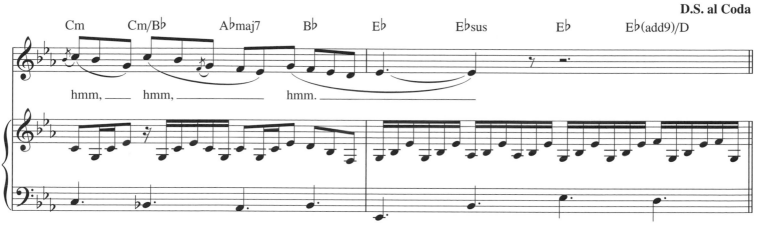

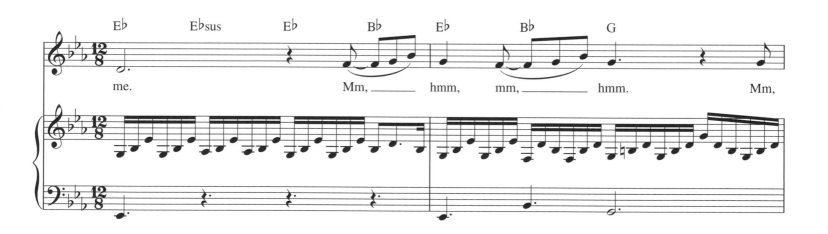

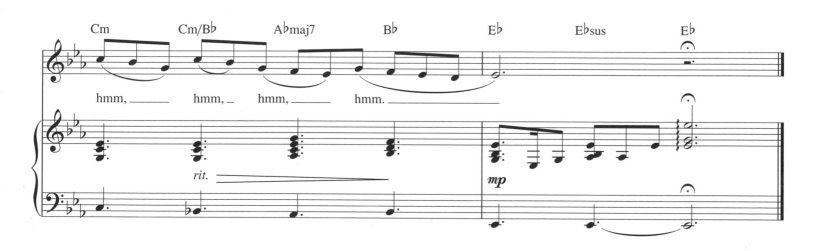

# Tell Her About It

Words and Music by Billy Joel

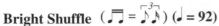

**Bright Shuffle**

Ooh, _____ ooh, ooh, _

ooh. _____

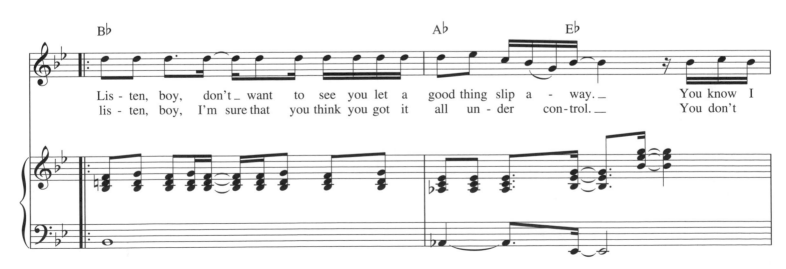

Lis-ten, boy, don't_ want to see you let a good thing slip a - way._ You know I
lis-ten, boy, I'm sure that you think you got it all un - der con-trol._ You don't

You know I
You don't

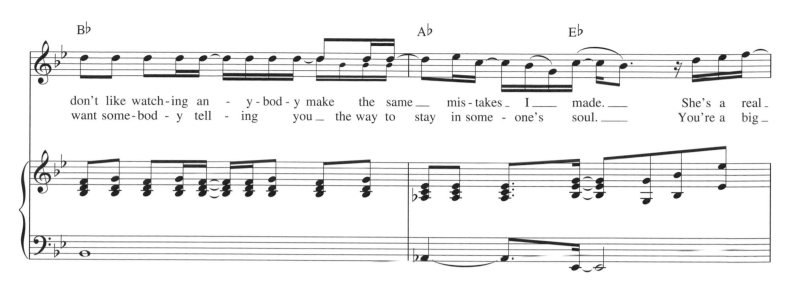

don't like watch-ing an - y-bod-y make the same _ mis-takes _ I _ made. _ She's a real _
want some-bod - y tell - ing you _ the way to stay in some - one's soul. _ You're a big _

_ nice girl _ and she's al - ways there for you. _ But a nice _
_ boy now _ and you'll nev - er let her go. _ But that's just _

_ girl would-n't tell _ you what _ you should do. _ Oh,
_ the kind of thing _ she ought _ to know. _

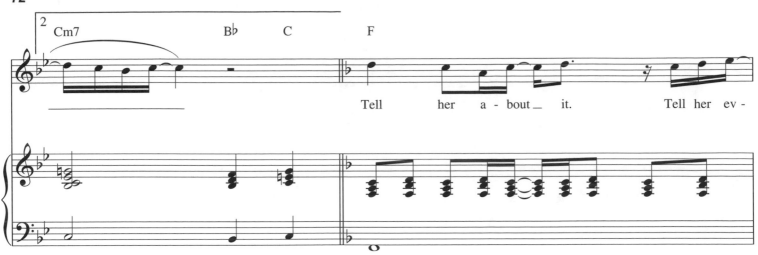

Tell her a - bout _ it. Tell her ev -

- 'ry - thing you feel. _____ Give her ev - 'ry rea - son to ac -

cept that you're for real. _____ Tell her a - bout _ it. Tell her all _

your cra - zy dreams. _____ Let her know_ you need_ her. Let her know_

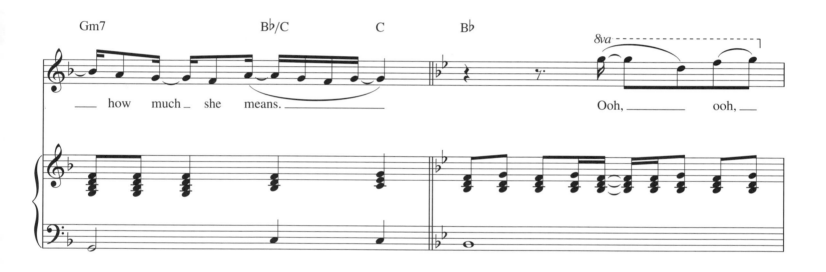

how much_ she means. _____ Ooh, _____ ooh, ___

ooh, _ ooh, ooh. _

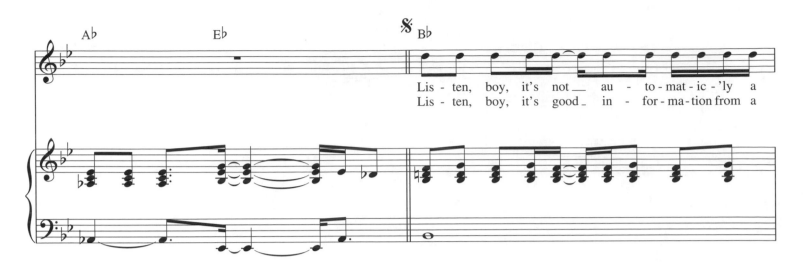

Lis - ten, boy, it's not __ au - to - mat - ic - 'ly a
Lis - ten, boy, it's good __ in - for - ma - tion from a

cer - tain guar - an - tee. __ To in - sure your - self, you've got __ to pro - vide com - mu - ni -
man who's made __ mis - takes. __ Just a word __ or two __ that she gets __ from you could be the

ca - tion con - stant - ly. __ When you love __ some - one __ you're al - ways in - se - cure.
dif - f'rence that it makes. __ She's a trust - ing soul, __ she's put her trust in you. __

And there's on - ly one good way to re - as - sure.
But a girl like that won't tell you what_ you should do.__

Tell her a - bout_ it. Let her know_
Tell her a - bout_ it. Tell her ev -

__ how much you care._____ When she can't_ be with_ you, tell her
- 'ry thing you feel._____ Give her ev - 'ry rea - son to ac -

you wish you were there._____ Tell her a - bout\_ it ev -'ry day\_
cept that you're for real._____ Tell her a - bout\_ it. Tell her all\_

\_\_\_ be - fore\_ you leave._____ Pay her some\_ at - ten - tion. Give her some -
\_\_\_ your cra - zy dreams._____ Let her know\_ you need\_ her. Let her know\_

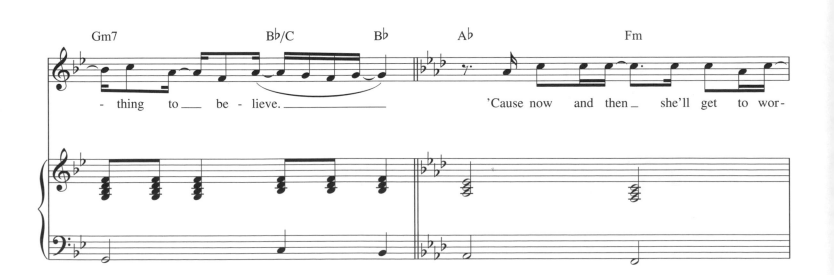

- thing to \_\_\_ be - lieve._____ 'Cause now and then\_ she'll get to wor-

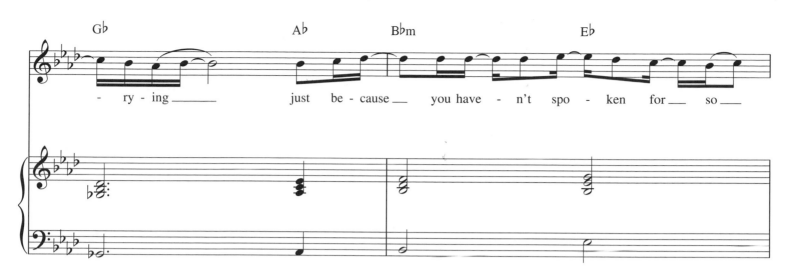

-ry - ing _____ just be - cause _____ you have - n't spo - ken for _____ so _____

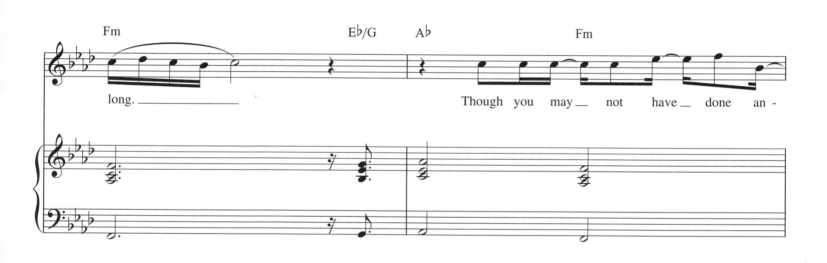

long. _____ Though you may _____ not have _____ done an -

- y - thing, _____ will that be a con - so - la - tion when _____ she's _____

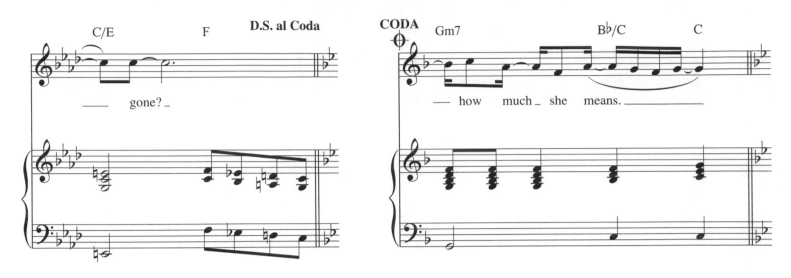

**D.S. al Coda**

C/E      F

\_\_ gone? \_

**CODA**  Gm7        Bb/C    C

\_ how much \_ she means. \_\_\_\_

Bb

Tell      her  a - bout \_ it.
tell      her  a - bout \_ it.

Ab           Eb

Tell her how \_ you feel \_ right  now. \_ Just
Tell her now \_ and you won't \_ go  wrong. \_ You got to

Bb

tell      her  a - bout \_ it.
tell      her  a - bout \_ it.

**1.**
Ab           Eb

The  girl  don't  want  to  wait \_ too \_ long. \_ You got to
Be -

fore it gets _ too late, _ you got _ to tell her a - bout _ it. You know, the

girl don't want _____ to wait. _____ You got _____ to

tell her a - bout _ it. You got to tell, tell, tell _ her a - bout _ it. Now,

**Repeat and Fade**

The Keyboard Play-Along series will help you quickly and easily play your favorite songs as played by your favorite artists. Just follow the music in the book, listen to the CD to hear how the keyboard should sound, and then play along using the separate backing tracks. The melody and lyrics are also included in the book in case you want to sing, or simply to help you follow along. The audio CD is playable on any CD player. For PC and Mac users, the CD is enhanced so you can adjust the recording to any tempo without changing pitch! Each book/CD pack in this series features eight great songs.

## 1. POP/ROCK HITS
Against All Odds (Take a Look at Me Now) (Phil Collins) • Deacon Blues (Steely Dan) • (Everything I Do) I Do It for You (Bryan Adams) • Hard to Say I'm Sorry (Chicago) • Kiss on My List (Hall & Oates) • My Life (Billy Joel) • Walking in Memphis (Marc Cohn) • What a Fool Believes (The Doobie Brothers).
00699875 Keyboard Transcriptions ..........................................................$14.95

## 2. SOFT ROCK
Don't Know Much (Aaron Neville) • Glory of Love (Peter Cetera) • I Write the Songs (Barry Manilow) • It's Too Late (Carole King) • Just Once (James Ingram) • Making Love Out of Nothing at All (Air Supply) • We've Only Just Begun (Carpenters) • You Are the Sunshine of My Life (Stevie Wonder).
00699876 Keyboard Transcriptions ..........................................................$12.95

## 3. CLASSIC ROCK
Against the Wind (Bob Seger) • Come Sail Away (Styx) • Don't Do Me like That (Tom Petty and the Heartbreakers) • Jessica (Allman Brothers) • Say You Love Me (Fleetwood Mac) • Takin' Care of Business (Bachman-Turner Overdrive) • Werewolves of London (Warren Zevon) • You're My Best Friend (Queen).
00699877 Keyboard Transcriptions ..........................................................$14.95

## 4. CONTEMPORARY ROCK
Angel (Sarah McLachlan) • Beautiful (Christina Aguilera) • Because of You (Kelly Clarkson) • Don't Know Why (Norah Jones) • Fallin' (Alicia Keys) • Listen to Your Heart (D.H.T.) • A Thousand Miles (Vanessa Carlton) • Unfaithful (Rihanna).
00699878 Keyboard Transcriptions ..........................................................$12.95

## 5. ROCK HITS
Back at One (Brian McKnight) • Brick (Ben Folds) • Clocks (Coldplay) • Drops of Jupiter (Tell Me) (Train) • Home (Michael Buble) • 100 Years (Five for Fighting) • This Love (Maroon 5) • You're Beautiful (James Blunt)
00699879 Keyboard Transcriptions ..........................................................$14.95

## 6. ROCK BALLADS
Bridge over Troubled Water (Simon & Garfunkel) • Easy (Commodores) • Hey Jude (Beatles) • Imagine (John Lennon) • Maybe I'm Amazed (Paul McCartney) • A Whiter Shade of Pale (Procol Harum) • You Are So Beautiful (Joe Cocker) • Your Song (Elton John).
00699880 Keyboard Transcriptions ..........................................................$14.95

## 7. ROCK CLASSICS
Baba O'Riley (The Who) • Bloody Well Right (Supertramp) • Carry on Wayward Son (Kansas) • Changes (David Bowie) • Cold As Ice (Foreigner) • Evil Woman (Electric Light Orchestra) • Space Truckin' (Deep Purple) • That's All (Genesis).
00699881 Keyboard Transcriptions ..........................................................$14.95

## 11. THE DOORS
Break on Through to the Other Side • Hello, I Love You (Won't You Tell Me Your Name?) • L.A. Woman • Light My Fire • Love Me Two Times • People Are Strange • Riders on the Storm • Roadhouse Blues.
00699886 Keyboard Transcriptions ..........................................................$14.95

## 12. CHRISTMAS HITS
Baby, It's Cold Outside (Tom Jones & Cerys Matthews) • Blue Christmas (Elvis Presley) • Merry Christmas, Darling (Carpenters) • Mistletoe and Wine (Cliff Richard) • Santa Baby (Eartha Kitt) • A Spaceman Came Travelling (Chris de Burgh) • Step into Christmas (Elton John) • Wonderful Christmastime (Paul McCartney).
00700267 Keyboard Transcriptions ..........................................................$14.95

FOR MORE INFORMATION,
SEE YOUR LOCAL MUSIC DEALER,
OR WRITE TO:

**HAL•LEONARD®**
CORPORATION
7777 W. BLUEMOUND RD. P.O. BOX 13819
MILWAUKEE, WISCONSIN 53213

Prices, contents, and availability subject to change without notice.